About the Author

Andy has taught science and mathematics across both primary and secondary phases for over 34 years. In this time Andy has widely published in both scientific and educational journals. His current interests lie in educational research that is focused upon STEM education and inter-disciplinary education.

Dedication

This book is dedicated to my mother (Lilian) and father (David) who provided me with the most wonderful childhood in Cornwall.

ANDY MARKWICK

A Cornish Tale

Austin Macauley Publishers
LONDON * CAMBRIDGE * NEW YORK * SHARJAH

Copyright © Andy Markwick (2019)

The right of Andy Markwick to be identified as author of this work has been asserted by him in accordance with section 77 and 78 of the Copyright, Designs and Patents Act 1988.

All rights reserved. No part of this publication may be reproduced, stored in a retrieval system, or transmitted in any form or by any means, electronic, mechanical, photocopying, recording, or otherwise, without the prior permission of the publishers.

Any person who commits any unauthorised act in relation to this publication may be liable to criminal prosecution and civil claims for damages.

A CIP catalogue record for this title is available from the British Library.

ISBN 978-1-78878-929-5 (Paperback)
ISBN 978-1-78878-930-1 (Hardback)
ISBN 978-1-52895-640-6 (ePub e-book)

www.austinmacauley.com

First Published (2019)
Austin Macauley Publishers Ltd
25 Canada Square
Canary Wharf
London
E14 5LQ

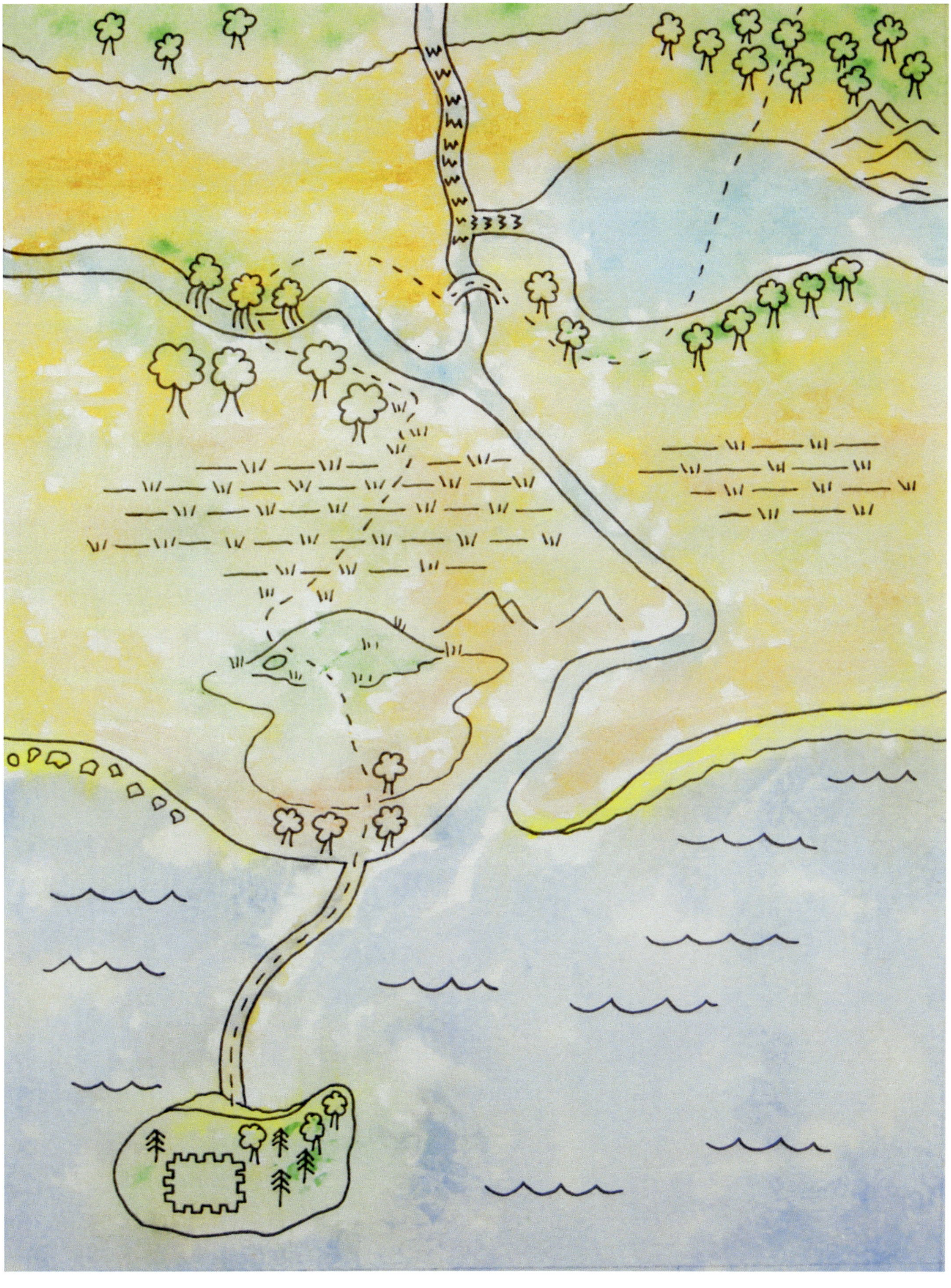

Codes

C = Calculation

I = Investigation

R = Research

T = Text

G = Grammar

** = Teachers' guide and additional worksheets are available from
www.stemconsultancy.co.uk

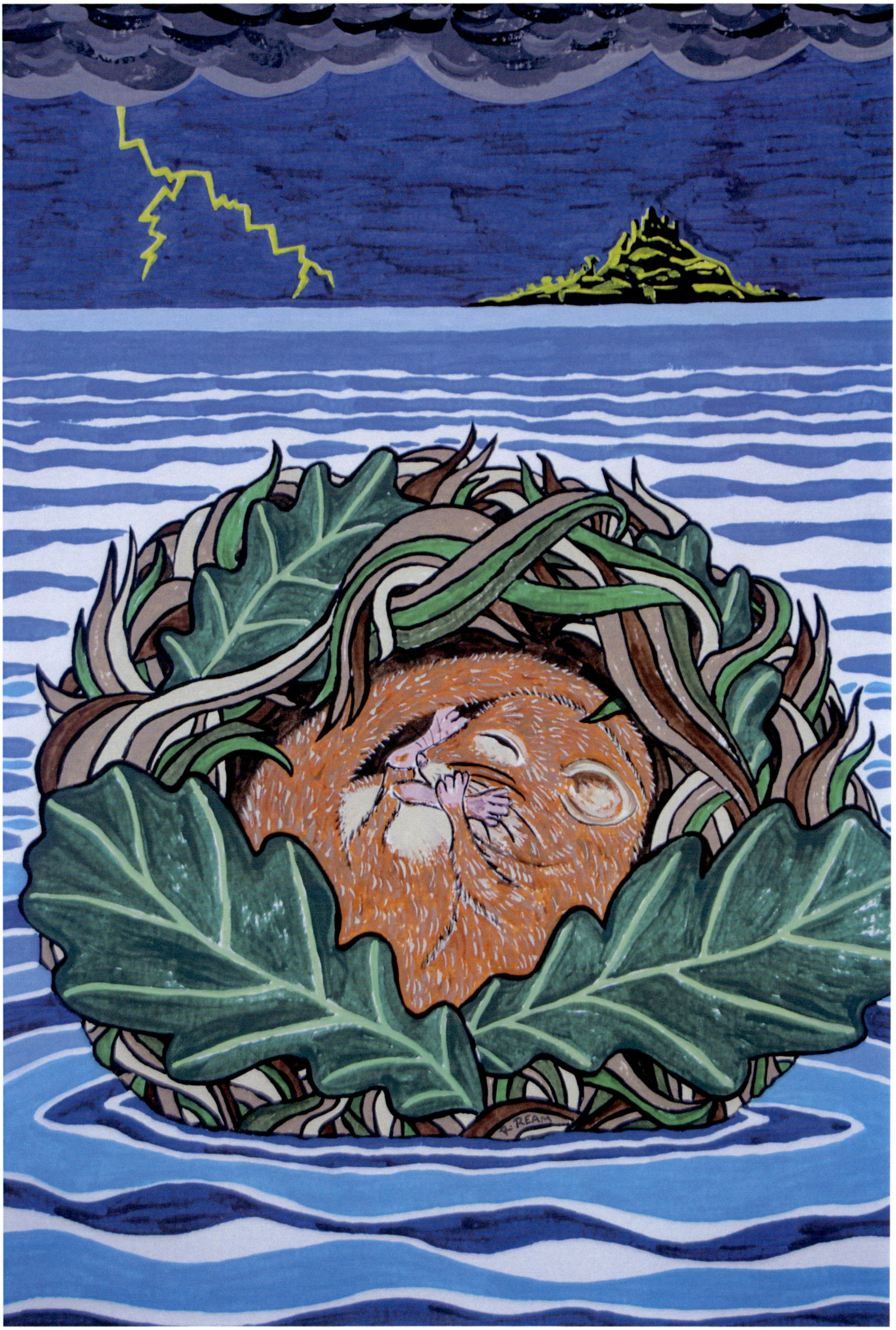

THE THUNDERSTORM

The sun was setting, lazily slipping below the horizon to rest until another dawn.

Tegan, the dormouse, began to drift into a sweet, deep sleep. Nothing would wake him now, not even the thunderstorm that was gathering high in the darkening sky!

Deafening cracks, slaps and flashes of blinding lightning filled the sky, yet Tegan did not wake.

The rain began to fall. At first small drops fell, patting the ground softly, but soon these drops coalesced into large blobs that splashed and slapped into the ground. Still, Tegan slept deeply.

So much rain fell that the river Dowr Tamarind began to swell and rise and within twenty minutes its banks burst open and the river was free.

Water flooded into the wood, Derowen Koes, and slowly and menacingly crept towards Tegan's home; a small hole in the base of an old oak tree. The oldest and largest tree in Derowen Koes.

The flood water began to lift Tegan's bed of twigs and leaves and swept it silently towards the swift, booming Tamarind.

Tegan was dreaming about eating nuts and seeds and sleeping, because that's what he liked to do.

He was unaware that the Tamarind water was rushing him away from his oak tree home and towards the deep sea.

Science:
a) R What does a dormouse look like? How big is a dormouse?

b) R What does an oak tree look like?

c) R How are thunder and lightning made?

d) I Static electricity **

STEM:
Make a raft for Tegan. Test your raft. **

Mathematics:
a) I Measuring leaves **

b) C It takes the earth 24 hours to rotate on its axis. This is an earth day. Calculate how many minutes and seconds this would be. Jupiter has a day lasting 10 hours. Calculate how many minutes and seconds its day is.

d) C A dormouse has a mass of about 130g, a human's mass is about 62,000g and an elephant's mass is 6,000,000g. Calculate the difference in mass between a dormouse and a human. How many dormice would be needed to equal the mass of an elephant?

English:
a) T How many words can you make from (i) thunderstorm (ii) tamarind (iii) dormouse?

b) T What is the longest word you can make from menacingly?

c) G Underline all nouns in the following sentence

The flood water began to lift Tegan's bed of twigs and leaves and swept it silently towards the swift, booming Tamarind.

d) G Underline all verbs in the following sentence

The rain began to fall. At first small drops fell, patting the ground softly, but soon these drops coalesced into large blobs that splashed and slapped into the ground. Still, Tegan slept deeply.

e) G Re-write the following sentence correctly

the causeway, when submerged was a Home for a variety of interesting creatures, including muscles, periwinkles that gripped onto its sides it was a shelter for fish and an attachment point for seaweed that bobbed up and down along the edge of the causeway

f) R Explain in 200 words, why a dormouse might choose to live in an oak tree?

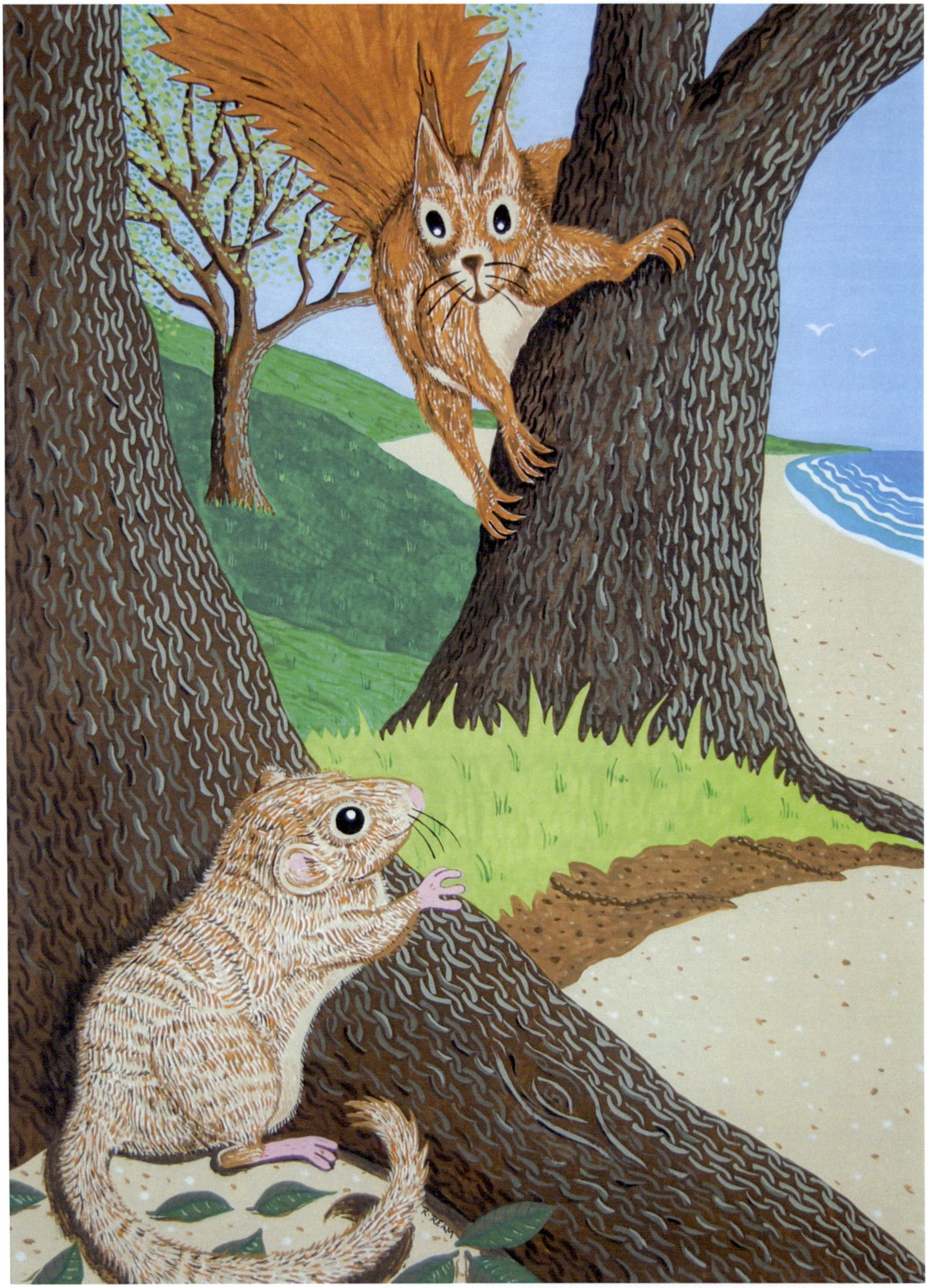

WAKING UP ON THE MOUNT

The sun had begun to peek above the horizon, shooting out intense beams of golden light that cut through the night sky and gently nudged Tegan awake. It was morning and Tegan, who had slept beautifully, stretched out his tiny legs and yawned a surprisingly large yawn for such a small creature. He felt great, until his eyes were fully opened.

Where was he? Was he still dreaming? What was this place? He didn't recognise it at all. Where was his oak tree?

Tegan was confused and could feel a tingle of panic move through his body; he was a little scared. His bed had been washed onto the sandy beach of The Mount; a small island off the mainland. Tegan could see the mainland, but no way of getting back there. He was marooned!

As usual Tegan had woken up very hungry. His tiny tummy was empty! Looking around him, he saw a copse of ash and hazel trees and thought, FOOD, I must investigate!

As he approached the boundary of the copse he heard a rustle and snap from high in the canopy. He remained motionless, just in case he was in danger. His small orange-brown body blended in perfectly with the floor of fallen leaves, earth and twigs.

It was just then that he spied a rather acrobatic and very red squirrel, with an enormous bushy tail, leaping from one branch to another.

"Hello down there, I've not seen you in these parts before. Are you visiting?" said the squirrel as she darted from one tree to another.

"No," cried Tegan, "I'm lost and I really miss my oak tree. I must get home because my family will be worried".

"Oh dear," said the squirrel. "Maybe I can help you get home. My name is Aife Dearg, The Fearless. What is your name and what are you?"

"I'm called Tegan and I'm a dormouse and I'm a little scared. Can you really help me to get home?"

"Well, that depends on where you live," said Aife with a chuckle.

"I live in my old oak tree in Derowan Koes," said Tegan.

"Ah, I've heard of this place. It's across the water and far to the north-west. I am sure that with the help of my friends we can get to your home," Aife said confidently. Aife looked at the position of the sun and said, "We will set off in about an hour, which should give us enough time to prepare for our journey ahead."

Science:

a) R How do predators and prey use camouflage?

b) R What would a squirrel find edible from ash and hazel trees?

c) R What other plants and animals might live in this copse?

d) R Investigate the history of red squirrels in the UK and across the world.

STEM:

Design, make and test a ladder or similar equipment for Tegan to reach the food at the top of a tree.

Mathematics:

a) I Using a compass, find North West from your classroom. R What towns and cities could you visit if you travelled NW from your classroom?

b) I Design a sundial that tells the time using the position of the Sun. **

c) R Find out how numbers of red squirrels have changed in the UK.

d) C Calculate the height of a tree.**

e) C The average height of an oak tree is 40m. A grey squirrel can leap 1.8m vertically. Calculate how many leaps it would take for the squirrel to reach the tree top.

f) C The mass of a red squirrel is about 330g, a grey squirrel has a mass of 600g. What is the difference in their masses?

g) C It is estimated that there are 2,000,000 grey squirrels and 120,000 red squirrels in the UK. How many more grey squirrels are there than red squirrels? What is the total mass (in kg) of red + grey squirrels in the UK?

English:

a) T Describe a time when you were afraid. What did you feel?

b) T Write a poem about the seaside (include sounds, sights, smells and feelings).

c) G Using expanded noun phrases and alliteration, write a paragraph that describes the sea in a thunderstorm.

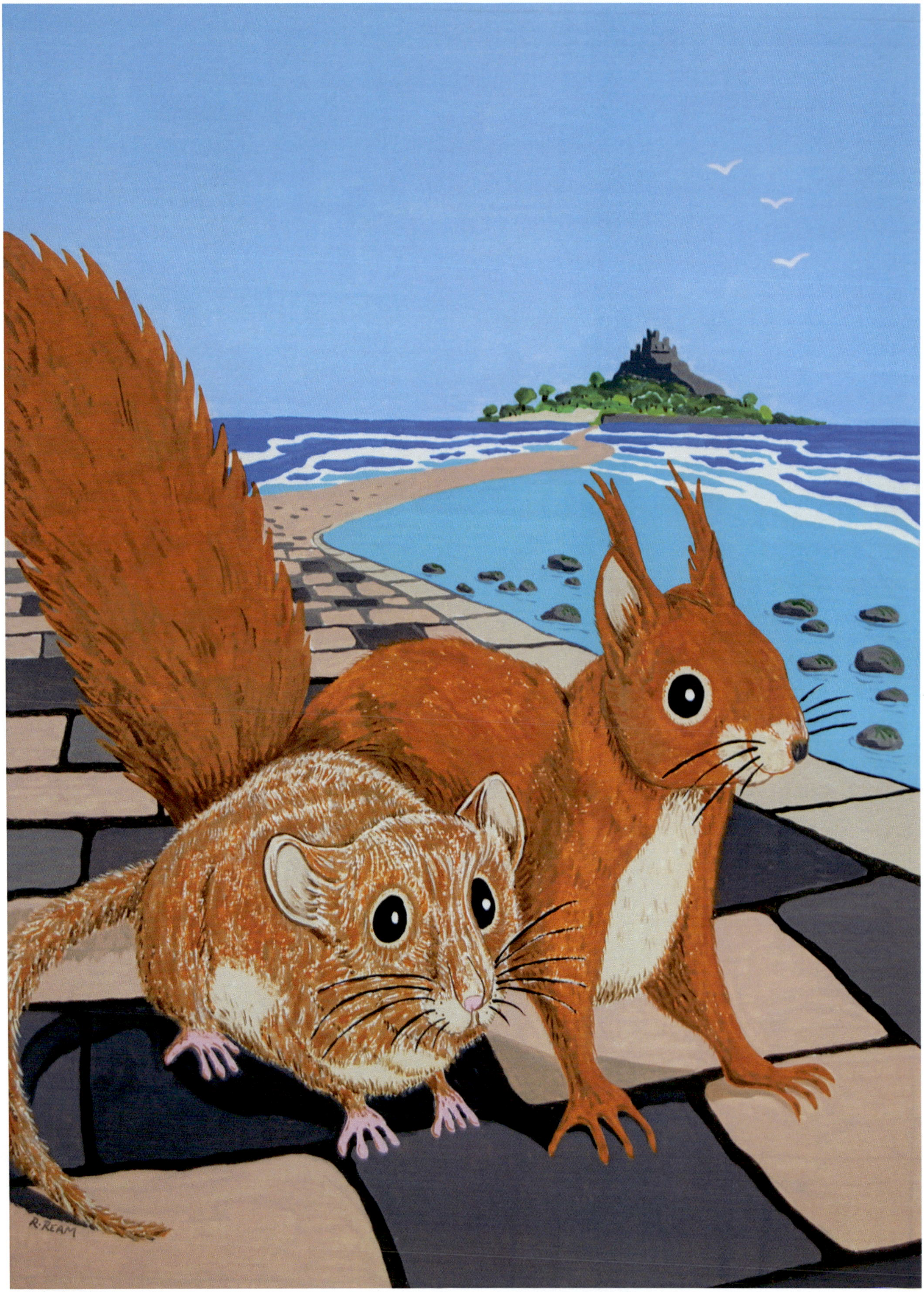
R. REAM

WALKING ON WATER

"How will we ever cross the water to get to the mainland? I can't swim and certainly can't walk on water!" exclaimed Tegan.

"Be patient and you will see," said Aife with a big grin on her face.

Sure enough, very slowly, a wet, glistening pink granite causeway was revealed as the tide fell. Tegan could not believe his eyes. "Is it safe to walk across? It looks very slippery," said Tegan.

The causeway, when submerged, was home to a variety of interesting creatures, including mussels and periwinkles that gripped onto its sides. It was a shelter for fish and an attachment point for seaweed that bobbed up and down along the edge of the causeway.

"Hurry," said Aife, "We must cross the causeway before the tide turns. It will be safe as long as we tread carefully and stay away from the edge."

The two new friends sped across the slippery granite as fast as they could until they reached the mainland. High above they heard Goelann the seagull and her rather loud and screechy friends discussing whether the pair would beat the tide and make it to the other side.

They had only just made it. Looking back Tegan could not see the causeway on The Mount side, the tide had risen once again.

Tegan had never seen the sea before. He was fascinated by the sounds of the splashing waves, the deafening seagull conversations and the smell of the salty sea water.

"I think we should rest here for tonight," said Aife. "We have a long way to go and will need our strength to cross the Kosel Marsh."

Science:

a) **R** What causes high and low tide?

b) **R** Investigate the seaside habitat (Flora and Fauna) and produce a poster.

c) **I** Investigate which rock is most slippery when wet. ******

STEM:

Design, make and test a material that could be used to make Tegan a non-slip pair of shoes to cross the causeway.

Mathematics:

a) **C** Times of the tides ******

b) **C** Heights of tides around the world. ******

English:

a) **G** Underline all adjectives in the following sentence

Lowarn sniffed the air and listened for the slightest sound. He moved closer and closer towards Tegan. He could not see or hear him, but smelt something different in the air.

b) **T** Describe how you imagine the marsh to be at night.

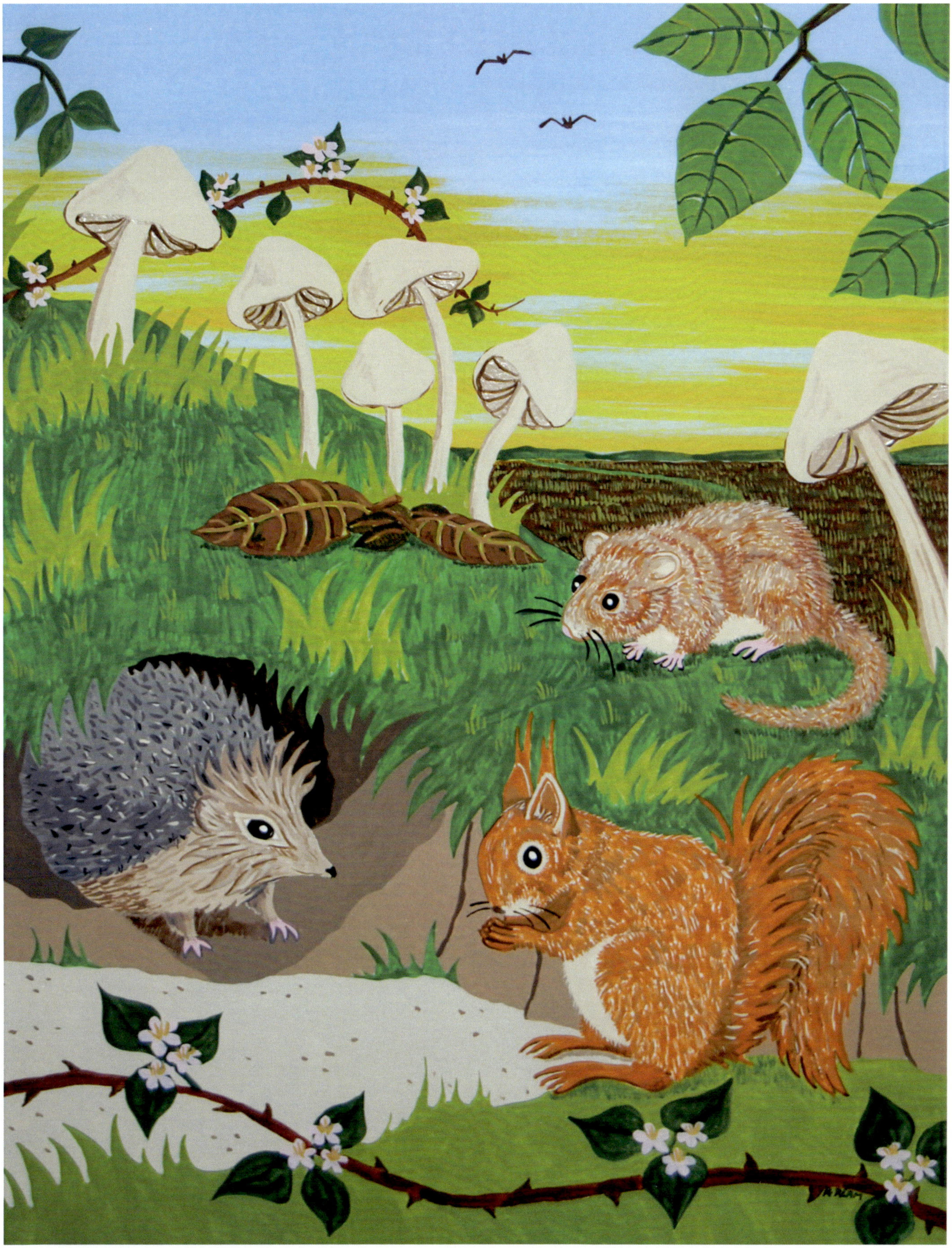

LOWARN AND SNUFFLES

Tegan, as you know, had little trouble falling asleep and even less with the hypnotic sounds of the slushing sea and the beautiful orange and red sunset.

He awoke very early, earlier than he normally liked to. Aife had been tickling his feet. She had tried everything to wake Tegan and found that this was the only way to stir him.

"Good morning Tegan," said Aife. "I hope you are well rested and ready for our adventure."

Aife had been up for several hours and using her acute sense of smell, found a range of seeds and nuts to take with them on their journey. She packed these into a small basket she made from twigs and leaves.

It was now time to set off towards Kosel Marsh. Before they ventured into the marsh, the friends needed to rendezvous with Snuffles the hedgehog for some important information.

Snuffles lived on Hedgehog Hill, at the edge of the marsh. He knew the marsh well.

> **English:** Discuss what important information Snuffles might have?

The air was crisp and refreshing, and the icy ground crunched underfoot. It was a good day to walk across the meadow amongst the early-rising snowdrops and crocus.

"How long will it take to reach Hedgehog Hill?" said Tegan impatiently.

"At our pace, about two hours I would say," replied Aife.

As they walked and spoke Aife's keen hearing picked up a rustle in the distance.

"Quiet," said Aife. "There is something in the long grass ahead of us."

Tegan had an acute sense of smell and began to sniff the air. Suddenly he caught an unfamiliar odour.

"What is it?" cried Tegan.

"It's Lowarn, the fox. We must be quiet; he is looking for his next meal," whispered Aife.

"I will climb that horse chestnut; it will give me a good vantage point and I will be safe. You must stay motionless Tegan and hope he doesn't sniff you out!"

Aife darted up the tree in a flash of red and Tegan froze on the spot. Tegan's orange-brown fur superbly camouflaged him against the ground. He became almost invisible!

Lowarn sniffed the air and listened for the slightest sound. He moved closer and closer towards Tegan. He could not see or hear him, but smelt something different in the air.

"This scent is unusual, it appears to be squirrel, yet there is something different about it," thought Lowarn to himself.

Lowarn was only ten centimetres from Tegan when he was startled by a scream coming from a nearby horse chestnut tree.

"Hey you, Lowarn the fox!"

"I'm up in the tree and you can't get me," screamed Aife at the top of her voice.

Lowarn was puzzled.

"You have an unusual scent little squirrel, not one I have encountered before," said Lowarn.

"Yes, I'm an unusual squirrel. I am Aife Dearg, The Fearless; you don't scare me Lowarn!"

"Are you alone fearless one?" asked Lowarn in a menacing tone.

"Of course. You should not waste your time with me, because in this tree you can't reach me," said Aife.

Lowarn was far too hungry to wait for his dinner to come to him and so he began to reluctantly move slowly away in search of other prey.

From high in the tree, Aife could see Lowarn disappear into the distance. When she was sure she would no longer be a danger, she returned to the ground.

"Tegan, where are you?" said Aife.

Tegan's camouflage was so good that even Aife could not find him.

"I'm over here," said Tegan. "That was too close for comfort; I thought my time was up!"

"You were lucky, Lowarn seldom loses his prey! We must swiftly move away from here," said Aife with urgency in her voice.

"From my vantage point high in the horse chestnut tree, I had a clear view of Hedgehog Hill," said Aife. "It's not far from here, but we must hurry before Snuffles goes out to hunt for worms, beetles, caterpillars, earwigs and millipedes. He has a voracious appetite!"

Walking as fast as their little legs could carry them, both Tegan and Aife made good progress towards Hedgehog Hill.

As they approached the hill, Tegan, with his super-sense hearing, heard a snuffling sound emanating from a small circular and rather tidy hole in the side of Hedgehog Hill.

"Hello," cried Aife in a clear and friendly voice.

"Is that you young Aife?" replied Snuffles, as he poked his wet, wiggling nose out of the hole.

"It's been a while my friend," said Aife. "How are you?"

"Hungry!" replied Snuffles. "And who is this tiny creature?" said Snuffles inquisitively.

"Allow me to introduce my friend Tegan. Tegan is a dormouse from Derowen Koes. He has excellent camouflage and his hearing is quite remarkable!"

"What brings you to Hedgehog Hill? You are a long way from your home Tegan," said Snuffles.

Tegan told the story of the flood and their journey so far and of his need to return to his home.

"We need your guidance to safely cross Kosel Marsh," said Aife.

"I will help you to navigate the marsh, but first you must be aware of the dangers in the marsh," said Snuffles.

"The marsh is a beautifully quite place, where water-soaked soil is held together by reeds, rushes and sedges and the silence is only ever broken by the splishing, splashing and croaking sounds of frogs and toads. Many other creatures live in the marsh, but they are never heard and seldom seen. The marsh is a deceptive place. It has been said that the poorly prepared traveller may enter the marsh, yet may never leave it."

Snuffles continued to explain. "However, to safely cross Kosel Marsh you must follow the north-west path. This is a clear path, but you must ensure you walk on the tall tufts of sedges. Never leave the path, never step into the water-logged boggy patches and never travel through the marsh at night. To do this would be foolish. The bog would keep you!"

Both Tegan and Aife gulped.

"Anyway, I'm far too hungry to continue talking, I'm off to find food. Make yourself at home. I suggest that you collect what provisions you may need and ensure you start your journey at sunrise. Good to see you again young Aife, and nice to meet you Tegan," said Snuffles as he disappeared into the twilight.

Science:
a) **R** What other plants and animals might Tegan and Aife encounter in the marsh habitat?

b) **R** What are the differences between reeds, grasses, sedges and rushes?

c) **R** Hedgehogs are on the decline in the UK. Find out why this might be the case and make a display of what you find out.

STEM:
a) Design, make and test a basket to carry food in (use only twigs, leaves and string).

b) Could you build a home for Snuffles? What would you feed him?

> **Mathematics:**
>
> a) C Using the map of the marsh, find some food for Snuffles. **
>
> b) C A typical worm has a mass of 4g. Snuffles eats a third of his body mass every day. Snuffles has a mass if 1kg. How many worms would Snuffles need to eat each day?
>
> **English:**
>
> a) T Write about an interesting dream you have had or make up a story about an interesting dream you would like to have.
>
> b) T Write a sentence using onomatopoeia.

Sunrise came far too soon for Tegan. He could have done with several more hours of sleep. He was a dormouse after all!

After breakfast the friends set off through the marsh, making sure they kept to the tufts of grass and never stepping onto the squelchy, boggy ground.

Although Tegan and Aife followed Snuffle's instructions explicitly, walking through the marsh was slow-going. Twilight had begun to engulf them as they finally saw the edge of the marsh and heard the slow, purposeful roar of the wide, deep Dowr Tamarind. Images began to lose their colours, fading into shadowy greys with indistinct shapes.

As the darkness drew closer, Tegan could see small grey objects flitter in the air above his head. They swooshed and swished and filled the air with deafening, constant high-pitched chatter.

> **English:** Discuss what you think these animals might be? What is your evidence for this? What does nocturnal mean?

These were bats, hunting insects on the wing. Their acrobatic manoeuvres mesmerised both Aife and Tegan. They had never seen such a sight!

"We should rest here until morning," said Aife.

Tegan and Aife drifted into sleep.

Science:

a) R Bats are the only mammal that can fly. Investigate bat habitats and produce a display poster.

b) I Senses circus – practical. **

c) I Colour box – what colours fade most and least with fading light? **

STEM:

Design, build and test a waterproof and warm home for Snuffles. **

Mathematics:

a) C Is there a correlation between the mass and surface area of different leaves? **

b) C There are an estimated 1500 Greater Horseshoe bats in Cornwall. The average mass of a bat is 30g. Calculate the total mass of bats in Cornwall.

English:

a) T What adventures do you think Snuffles might have had when he left Aife and Tegan?

b) T Describe the home of Snuffles in any way you want to (writing, drawing, orally, making).

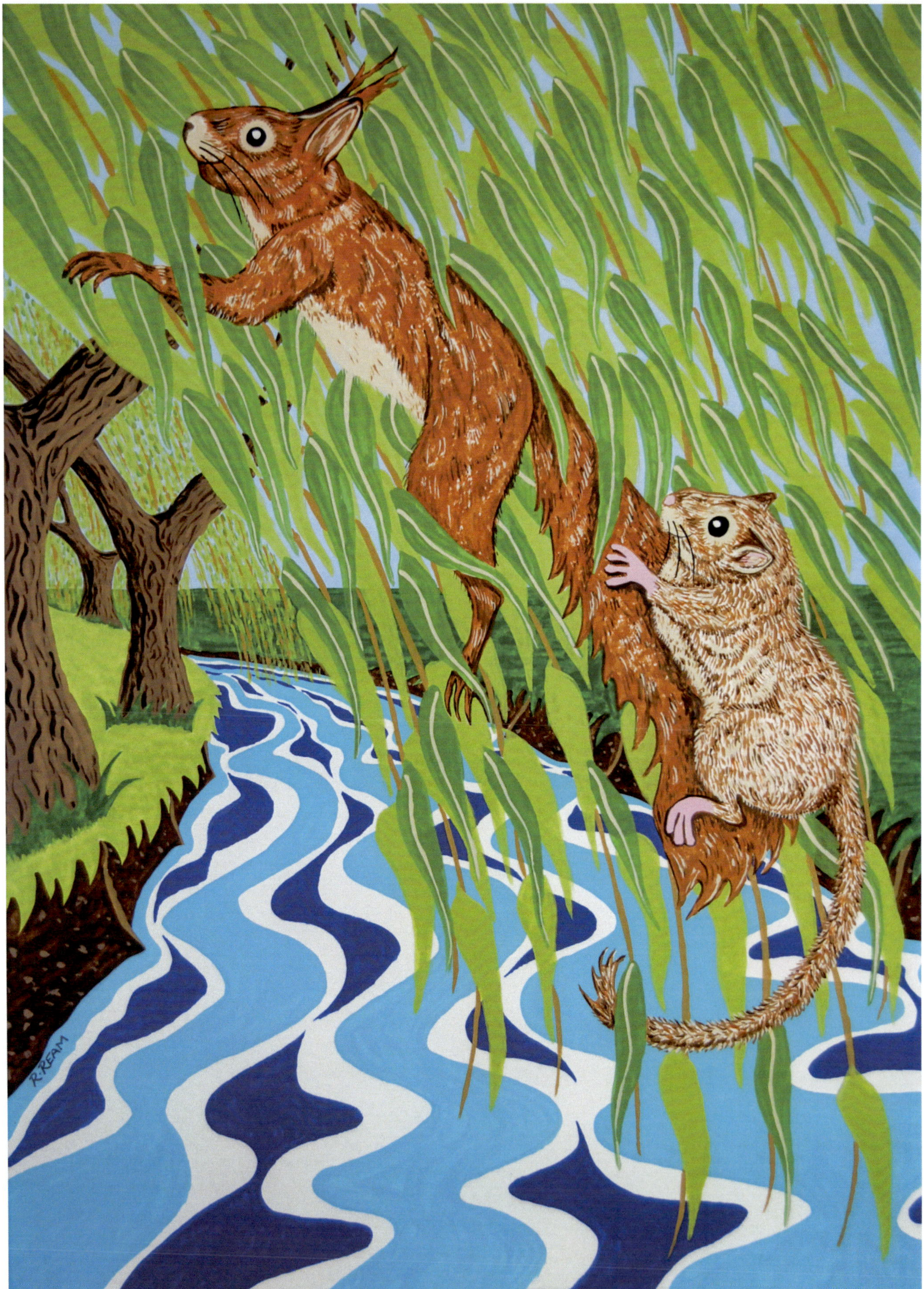
R. REAM

TOWARDS DOWR TAMARIND

"Where are we heading now?" asked Tegan. Aife explained that the next stage of their journey was to cross the Dowr Tamarind at Beaver's Bridge. However, before Snuffles had bade the friends farewell, he had mentioned the need to cross the small, yet sinuous Dowr Inny, which snaked its way through Dew Meadow.

The sounds of cascading water were in earshot and only a short distance across the meadow, a meadow filled with clumps of daisies and dandelions nestled within a carpet of thick, lush clover, a colourful and much welcomed feast for the two travellers as they romped towards the stream.

Dowr Inny was fast-flowing and far too deep to cross safely.

"Let's walk up-stream for a while to see if we can find a shallow spot to safely cross," said Aife.

They walked for quite some time listening to the stream move swiftly by, then suddenly, without warning, they saw streaks of red, yellow and blue flash before their eyes as if a colourful bolt of lightning had appeared from nowhere. The bolt entered the water without a splosh or splash and exploded into the air carrying a fish in its sharp, scissor-like beak.

It was Kennocha, the Kingfisher. Tegan was entranced by her beauty and agility.

"Welcome to my river, Aife and friend," said Kennocha. "What brings you here? You are not here to steal my fish, are you?" said Kennocha jokingly.

"Oh no, not fish, I don't like fish," said Tegan feeling rather ill at the thought of eating fish.

"That's ok then," said Kennocha giggling to herself.

"You are such a tease Kennocha," said Aife. "Can you help us get across your river? We are on our way to Beaver's Bridge."

"Well, I could carry your friend across the river in my beak, but you Aife, you are far too heavy!"

Tegan did not like the idea of being trapped in Kennocha's sharp beak and said very hesitantly, "Is there no other way of crossing your river…please?"

"There may be another way," said Kennocha thoughtfully. "There is a place up-stream called Helygen, where willow trees whisper in the breeze and drape their spindly branches across the river. You may be able to climb across the water there."

"Thank you Kennocha," said Aife. "We are in your debt."

The travellers hugged the western bank of Dowr Inny, as it snaked its way north, until they came across a meander in the river. "This must be Helygen," said Tegan excitedly.

Here a family of willow trees bowed their heads elegantly from one side of the river to the other.

Tegan and Aife grasped the thin willowy branches tightly and began to scramble over the water. Then suddenly Tegan lost his footing and began to fall. In a split second Aife flicked her tail towards Tegan and shouted, 'Grab hold of my tail Tegan, it's your only chance."

Without a second thought, Tegan gripped Aife's bushy red tail in both hands and was lifted to safety.

"Thank you Aife," said Tegan gratefully. "Your tail saved my life!"

It was now just a short distance from Beaver's Bridge and as its name implies, it was a sturdy prennek structure, built and maintained by a family of master-builder beavers. The bridge was a very impressive structure, straddling the entire width of Dowr Tamarind.

With a few hops, skips and jumps the friends managed to cross Beaver's Bridge to reach the eastern bank of Dowr Tamarind. The area became familiar to Tegan, he was almost home. One final challenge lay in front of them; Tala Water.

Science:

a) **R** What types of fish might live in Kennocha's river?

b) **R** What types of fish do kingfishers eat?

c) **R** What types of habitat do kingfishers like?

d) **R** What have willow trees been used for?

e) **R** The river Thames has changed its course. It used to flow out into the sea further north. Find out why this happened.

STEM:

Design and build a scale model of a beaver dam. ******

Mathematics:

a) **C** Kingfishers have a mass of about 40g. There are between 8,000 and 12,000 kingfishers in the UK. Calculate the total mass of kingfishers in the UK.

b) **R** What is the total distance of rivers? ******

c) **C** Imagine that the river Tamar in Cornwall flows with an average speed of 10km per hour. It is 98km long. How long would it take for a stick to float the full length (assume it doesn't get stuck or slowed down or speed up on its way).

English:

a) **T** As Tegan and Aife crossed the Beaver's Bridge they stopped to talk to the beavers. Write a conversation between Tegan, Aife and Beryle and Burty beaver.

b) **T** What challenges might Tegan and Aife meet as they travel towards Tala Water?

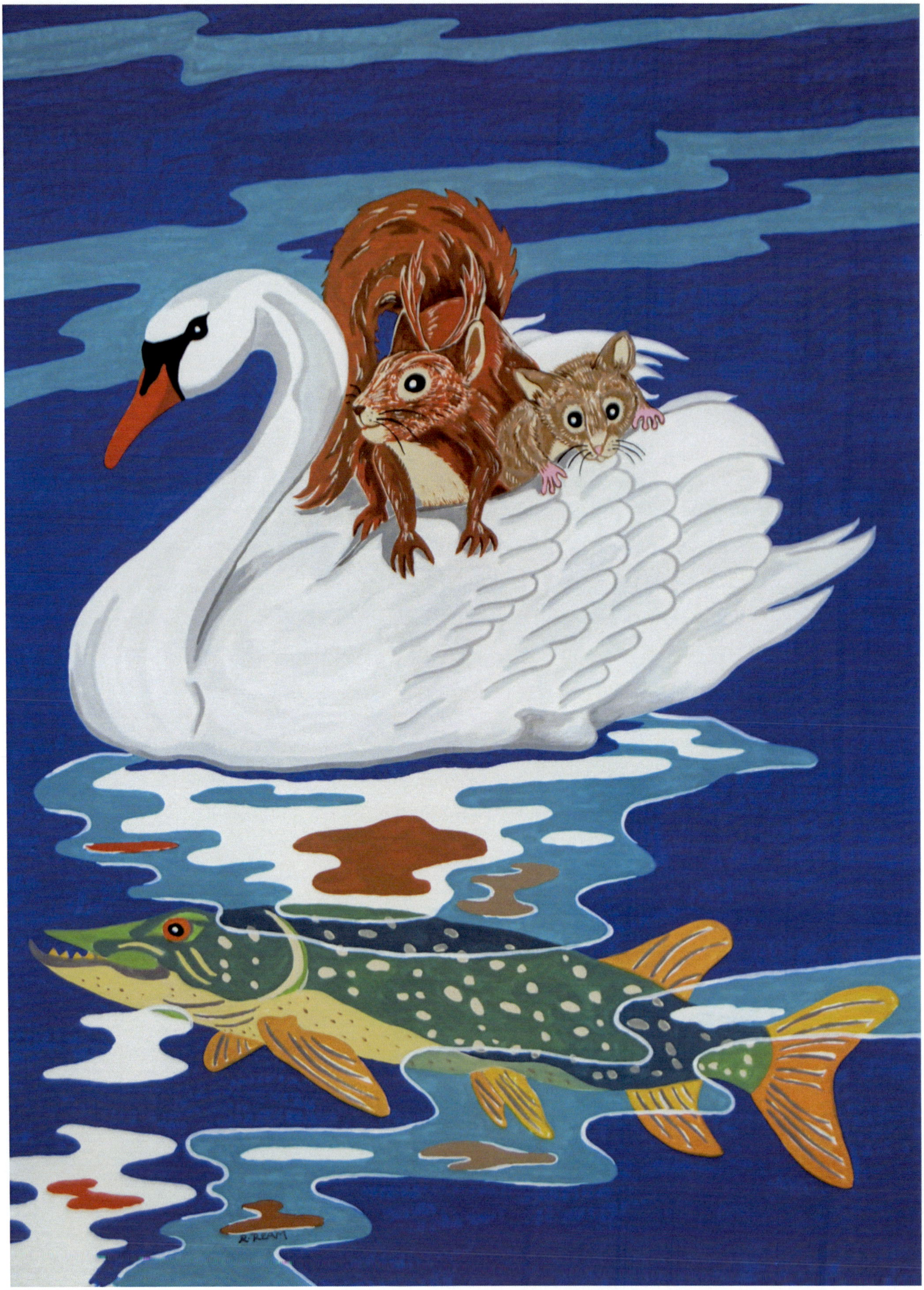

VOYAGE ACROSS TALA WATER

A symphony of colourful sound emanated from Tala Water as the breeze kissed the water's surface. This was a magical place thought Tegan, who had on many occasions visited the northern shore to visit his friend Alargh, a majestic swan whose beauty was almost impossible to imagine.

Crossing the Tala Water was not going to be easy. How could they cross such a vast expanse of water? They could not walk eastwards around the lake as it was bounded by the sheer cliffs of the Breow Hills, haunt of Eryon, king of the eagles and a fearsome hunter. Crossing the thundering Dowr Tamarind on the western side was out of the question. Then Tegan had an idea.

What if Alargh would agree to take them across the water? Tegan had always wanted to ride a white swan.

As they approached the lake's shore, Alargh could be seen effortlessly gliding across the water.

"Alargh my friend, how are you?" shouted Tegan.

Alargh's head turned gracefully towards him. "Well I never," said Alargh. "Where have you been young Tegan? Your family have been very worried about you. They thought they had lost you forever!"

Tegan briefly explained how he was swept away by the flood and how Aife and her friends had helped him to get home.

> **English:** To your partner, briefly recount Tegan's journey. What have been your favourite parts of the journey? What other adventures would you like Tegan and Aife to have?

"Can you help us get across the water?" asked Aife. "Indeed I can," said Alargh, "but I will want you to tell me your whole story on the way."

"I'd love to," replied Tegan with a smile in his heart.

Suddenly something caught Aife's eye as she looked skywards. She glimpsed a small black object soaring high above. "What is that?"

"That is Eryon, the eagle," said Alargh. "Be afraid. He looks far away, but don't be fooled. His eyes are keen and he sees everything. He can swoop down from high above in a blink of an eye. At this time of day he hunts so we must hide amongst the beech trees, protected from Eryon's gaze by the thick canopy of leaves. We will begin our voyage at dusk, only then can we safely cross Tala Water."

The friends headed towards the safety of Beech Koes. As they entered the Koes they saw, what appeared to be a beautiful blue-purple haze hugging the ground. It was May and that time of year when blue bells covered the woodland floor.

As dusk began to draw in the blue bell's colour began to change into an intense violet. It was time for Aife and Tegan to climb onto Alargh's extremely comfortable back. They were ready to sail. Neither Tegan nor Aife had sailed before. This was going to be an exciting experience.

The ride was surprisingly smooth, despite the water being choppy.

The friends were almost half-way across Tala Water when Aife glimpsed a faint, ghostly image that shimmered beneath them. It was the image of a very large and fearsome looking pike.

"That is Koth, they say she is the oldest and wisest creature in the lake. She lived in the lake even before the beech trees germinated," exclaimed Alargh.

"I bet she has some great stories to tell," said Tegan.

"That will have to wait until another time I believe," said Aife thoughtfully.

In the distance Tegan noticed a raft of mallard ducks hurrying towards their home, deep in the reeds, and a pair of coots noisily zig-zagging this way and that, as if they were unsure where to go.

They met the northern shore just as the sun began to force out shafts of intense yellow and white light. It was sunrise and Tegan could see the boundary of Derowan Koes, his home.

Tegan and Aife thanked Alargh for their sailing adventure and promised to meet her again soon.

"If you hurry you may make breakfast Tegan," said Alargh as she swiftly turned and headed back into Tala Water.

> **Science:**
>
> a) **R** Research the life cycle of a blue bell.
>
> b) **I** Look at the picture of the teeth of a pike. Is it a carnivore or herbivore. Explain. ******
>
> **STEM:**
>
> Make a floating home for the lake. It must have a garden. Include a boat to reach the mainland for supplies. ******
>
> **Maths:**
>
> a) **C** Mallards have around 11,900 feathers and swans have about 25,000 feathers. In the UK there are about 710,000 mallards and 79,000 swans. Calculate how many mallard and swan feathers there must be.
>
> b) **C** An average mallard feather has a mass of 0.0082g. Calculate the total mass of all Mallard duck feathers in the UK.
>
> **English:**
>
> a) **T** It's not commonly known, but the lake is home to a merman and mermaid. Write a story that describes their home.
>
> b) **R** Produce a poster that describes 5 interesting facts about mallard ducks.

HOME AT LAST

Tegan could smell home, well breakfast really. He was hungry, as usual, and very homesick. He wanted to see his family and to sleep in his own bed!

As the friends approached the great oak, they saw Tegan's rather large family run towards him and smother him in BIG HUGS AND KISSES. They were so pleased to see Tegan, they thought they might never see him again. The great oak stood towering before Tegan and Aife. "This is my home Aife, you are most welcome to stay with me as long as you want to," said Tegan.

"I thought we had lost you," said Tegan's mother with tears in her eyes. Tegan hugged his mum tightly and said, "My árth kar mother, I didn't think I would ever see you again, but I was so lucky to meet my new friend, Aife Dearg, The Fearless. She and her friends helped me to safely find my way home."

"Aife Dearg, you are most welcome in our home. We will always be indebted to you for looking after Tegan," said Tegan's mother humbly.

"Thank you. You are most welcome. Our adventure has been a prelude only. The real adventure is about to begin, if you want it to?" said Aife.

GLOSSARY

Characters	Meanings
Aife	Celtic name meaning "great warrior woman"
Dearg	Scottish word for 'red'
Alargh	Celtic name for swan
Eryon	Cornish name for eagles
Lowarn	Cornish name for fox
Kennocha	Cornish word for lovely
Tegan	Welsh name for "loved one"
Goelann	Cornish name for seagull
Koth	Cornish for old or eldest

Place names	Meaning
Derowen	Cornish for oak tree
Koes	Cornish for wood
Tala	A style of rhythmic Indian music
Broew	Cornish for hills
Helygen	Cornish for willow trees
Kosel	Cornish name for marsh
Prennek	Cornish for wooden
My árth kar	Cornish for "I love you"